This book belongs to:

Inspired by my niece
Aria

First published in 2024
Text copyright © Tineka Vieira

ISBN: 9798322780380

All rights reserved.

No part of this publication may be reproduced, or transmitted in any form or by any means, including photocopying, recording, or other electronic or mechanical methods, without the prior written permission of the publisher.

HOW MUCH DOES MY AUNTIE LOVE ME?

by tineka Vieira

My auntie loves me more than...

all the tiny grains of sand on the beach...

and the most deliciously drippy ice cream on a hot summers day...

and more than a wiggly piggly loves sludgy mud...

and more than cheerfully happy storybook endings...

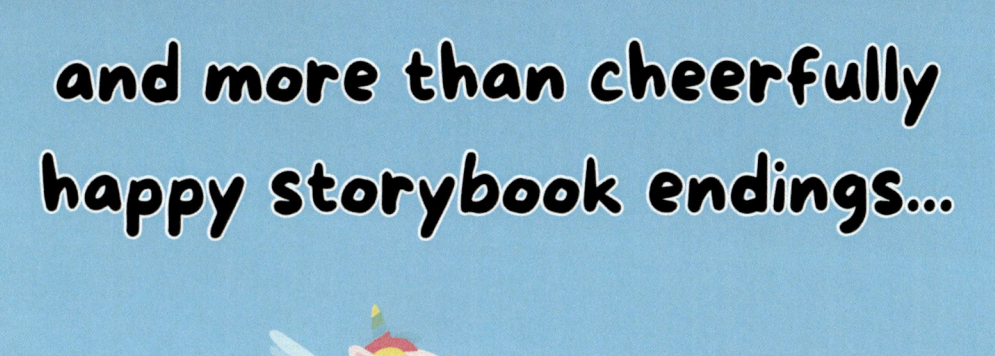

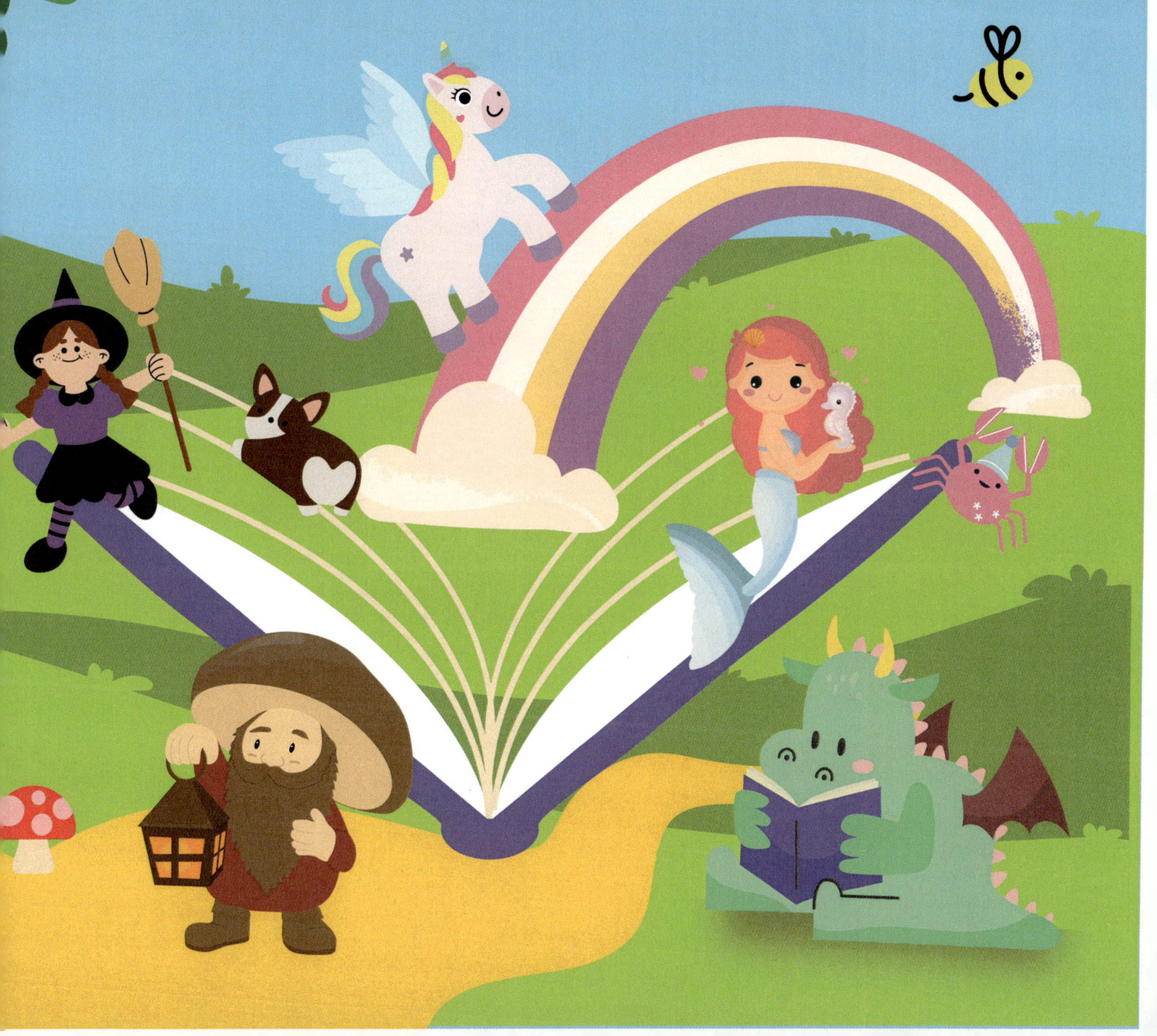

More than children love scrummy yummy candy...

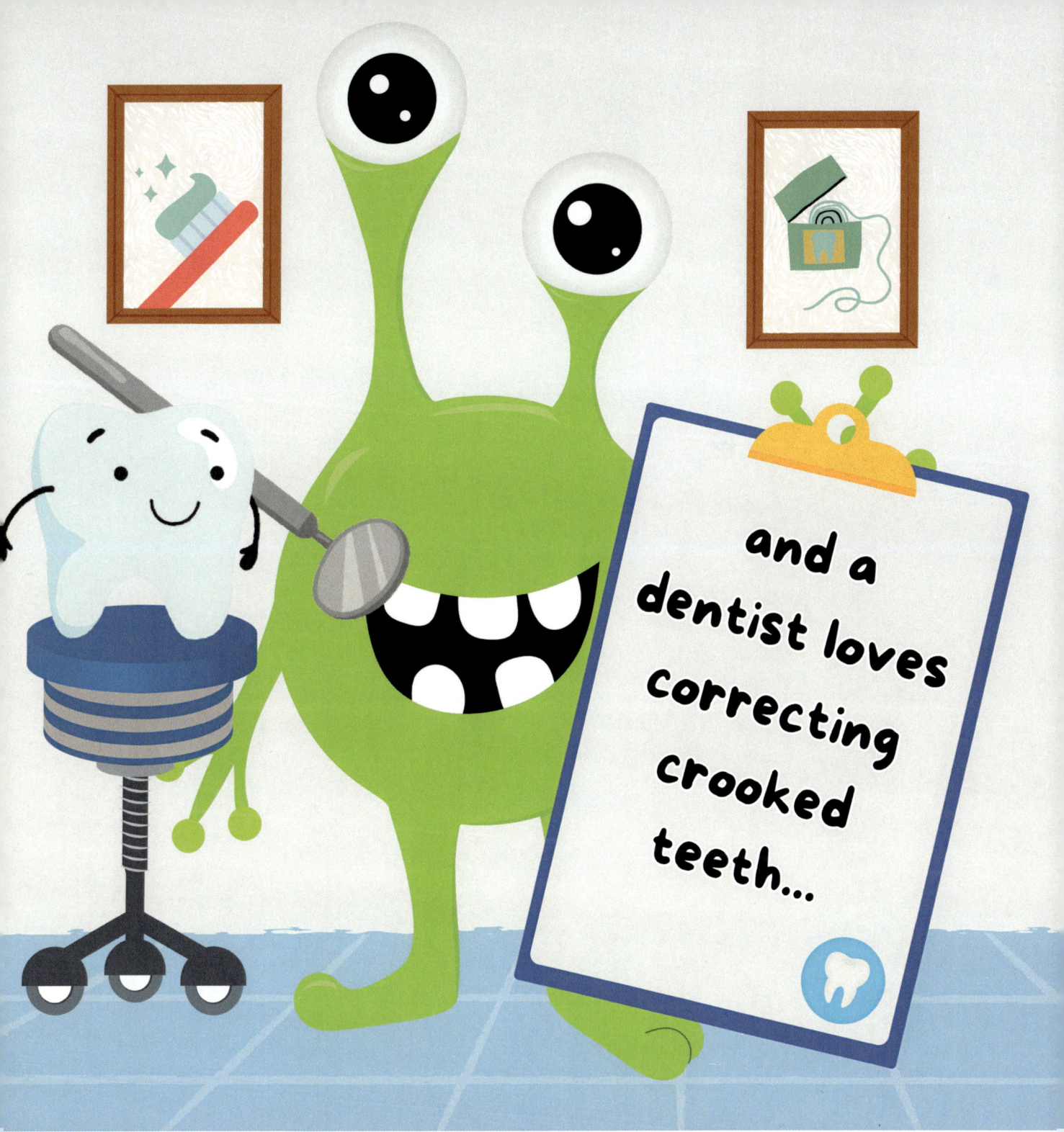

and the most splendiferous sunset...

and even more than 1 000 auntie cuddles would show me...

My auntie loves me more than all of the distance between us...

and her L♥VE for me will never change, no matter where I am...

Made in the USA
Las Vegas, NV
04 March 2025